52
Ways
to Encourage
Others

→» 52 «←
SIMPLE WAYS
· T O ·
ENCOURAGE
OTHERS

C. E. Rollins

A Division of Thomas Nelson Publishers
Nashville

To

Twila Allwine Eisley

who has been a steady source
of
encouragement and friendship
to me for more than
twenty years

Published in Nashville, Tennessee, by Oliver-Nelson Books, a
division of Thomas Nelson, Inc., Publishers, and distributed in
Canada by Lawson Falle, Ltd., Cambridge, Ontario.

Unless otherwise noted, the Bible version used in this publication is
THE NEW KING JAMES VERSION. Copyright © 1979, 1980, 1982,
Thomas Nelson, Inc., Publishers.

Printed in the United States of America.

Library of Congress Cataloging-in-Publication Data

Rollins, Catherine E., 1950–
    52 ways to encourage others / Catherine E. Rollins.
        p.   cm.
    ISBN 0-8407-9614-5
    1. Encouragement—Religious aspects—Christianity.   I. Title.
II. Title: Fifty-two ways to encourage others.
BV4647.E53R65   1992
241′.4—dc20   91-42117
                                                       CIP

1   2   3   4   5   6   —   97   96   95   94   93   92

♦ Contents

◆ Introduction

To encourage means literally to INcourage, to plant courage into another person—and thus, to help endow him or her with the necessary elements and strength for facing the present and the future with boldness and confidence. To encourage is to edify, to strengthen, to bolster.

Two vital ingredients of encouragement are these:

- *hope,* that the situation or circumstance will resolve itself into a good outcome and that the future will be better than the present;
- *faith,* which is the belief that the outcome for which you are hoping will come to pass.

To encourage others is to build up their reservoirs of hope and faith, to a great extent by sharing your inner reserves of these precious and God-inspired resources.

Encouragement is rooted in the positive. It is proactive and forward looking. The encouraging word is upbeat. Encouraging advice propels potential toward fulfillment. Encouragement seeks out what promotes healing and personal wholeness.

Encouragement is not only for those who are feeling "down and out" emotionally. It is for every person, no matter the emotional temperature or psychological landscape.

Ultimately, we must be encouraged before we can truly encourage others. And just as important, we must be able to share our encouragement. We must be able to communicate it.

Finally, encouragement is best framed within relationship. We might receive a "dose" of encouragement from a stranger or give an encouraging word to someone we meet in passing, but the better quality and more long-standing brand of encouragement comes on a day-in, day-out consistent basis from those who share life with us.

To be the best provider of encouragement, then, is to be a FRIEND (including being a friend even if you are also a relative or loved one). Moreover, the encouraging friend is faithful and loyal—not exchanging honesty for smarmy sentiment, but ever ready to provide a helping hand, a listening ear, and a loving heart. The encouraging friend is "there" when needed, without being asked, and is ever present in the heart of the other—no matter the physical distance—and ever ready to exert a presence that is positive and constant. Such a friendship is encouraging in and of itself! May each of us be such a friend.

Encouragement and love are not far apart. Both are grounded in giving, and both follow the principle that the more one gives, the more one receives. Be a generous provider of encouragement today. You'll feel more encouraged about life!

Things to Do

1 ♦ Meaningful Touch

The meaningful touch says, above all, "I'm here in a physical, tangible way to show my care, concern, and support." It may be

- a handshake.
- a tender kiss on the cheek.
- a giant bear hug.
- a gentle caress.
- a hand held in both of yours.
- a "high five" slap of hands.
- a tender embrace.
- a hand vigorously clasping a shoulder.

How to Touch   We all long to be touched or held when we are scared, feel alone, or have a sense of loss or estrangement. The meaningful touch conveys, "You are not alone in this. I'm here with you."

In touching others, we must be sensitive to the fact that truly "meaningful" touch is what is perceived as loving and positive by the person being touched. Some people have a great capacity for physical closeness. Others don't. What may be a touch of encouragement to one person may be a touch of embarrassment to someone else! How can you tell what type of touching is appropriate?

- Touch another person only to the extent he is capable of receiving your touch and returning it.

Does the person pull away from you, back away, turn away, or move to put an object between you? You've overstepped his bounds of appropriateness. If, on the other hand, the other person returns your hug or grasps both of your hands in hers, she is eager to receive more.

- Touch within the emotional context of the moment.

Has a friend just received word that a loved one has died? That person may need to be held in a strong hug for several moments in order to cry freely in the comfort of a strong embrace. The same type of hug, however, might be perceived as an inappropriate response to snagged hosiery or a bad day on the golf course. As a general rule, the greater the intensity of the emotions being expressed—the greater the loss, fear, or feeling of isolation—the greater the intensity of the touch.

- Touch within the restraint of friendship.

Don't allow your touch to excite or invite passion.

We are physical creatures. Our skin is the largest organ of our bodies. We respond to and need physical closeness for a feeling of physical well-being and wholeness. A touch says that we belong to the human community, that we are approachable and worthy to be included and loved.

A physical touch encourages another person by conveying, "You're O.K. You're one of us."

2 ◆ Provide a Place of Rest and Nurture

Anxiety—whether arising from enthusiasm for a new goal or challenge, from an impending major change in life, or from the loss of a relationship—often results in disrupted sleeping and eating patterns. Loss of sleep and lack of proper nourishment, in turn, can lead to a downward spiral resulting in depression or disorientation.

Often, the best "encouragement" you can give to a person is to provide a stable place where routine is maintained—where meals are served regularly, quiet prevails, and the atmosphere is marked by peace and a lack of confusion.

Food Do your best to provide meals high in food value—the freshest ingredients possible, balanced in protein and carbohydrate, and minimal caffeine and sugar. (Sugar often leads to energy highs and lows, which can be perceived by an anxious person as an emotional roller coaster. Caffeine is also a stimulant to many.) Bear in mind that the person needs building up; at the same time, don't expect the person to consume large quantities of food. Make the food as appealing in presentation as you can.

Rest If you or the person you are seeking to help has small children, try to make arrangements for them to visit friends during the day or to spend the night with relatives.

Exercise Encourage the person to exercise in moderation, to tune out the world (including the media), and to "play." Both the goal-oriented, task-driven person and the grieving, loss-stricken person tend to lose sight of the ability to have fun. Create an environment in which jokes are told. Play old parlor games. Seek out your favorite old black-and-white comedies on video. The more laughter the better!

Sometimes encouragement can be given by providing such a place of rest and nourishment for just a weekend. Indeed, a great deal can be said for a Saturday morning that operates according to this agenda: sleep until you wake, eat a hearty brunch, and take a brisk walk.

Strength As you provide nurture to another, be aware that a tendency toward codependency may develop. Don't enable another person to avoid life's challenges; help the individual to face life squarely! Look for signs that the person who is "discouraged" is becoming strong enough to help—such as to set the table or chop the ingredients for a salad—and to make decisions—for example, to plan an afternoon activity.

3 ♦ Send an Unexpected Uplifting Message

Find a way to say, "I'm glad you're in the universe the same time I am!" It might be

- a note tucked into a lunch box.
- a small jar of hard-candy hearts smuggled into an overnight bag.
- a card hidden in a briefcase.
- a message left on the answering machine.
- a note scribbled on a daily calendar.
- a message created by magnetic letters on the refrigerator.

Genuine Appreciation You don't need to buy an expensive greeting card or write a long treatise. A few words of genuine appreciation and affection scribbled on the outside of a brown paper lunch bag can be just as effective as a message engraved in stone.

You may want to write out a brief poem . . . a joke . . . or a verse of Scripture. (One fellow frequently finds riddles in his briefcase, with an added line: "Answer available at home!")

You don't even need to sign your name. Sometimes

it's fun to be a "secret pal" to someone who needs encouragement.

Encouragement The message doesn't need to be a love letter, although virtually any message of encouragement conveys love at some level. It might be a message that says simply,

- *"I believe in you!"*
- *"I'm praying that you'll do well on your math test."*
- *"Ten pounds down . . . wow!"*
- *"I miss seeing you."*
- *"Just wanted to say that I'm thinking about you. I hope things are going well for you."*
- *"Come home soon."*
- *"I feel blessed to have you as my friend."*

Send a message that doesn't require a reply.

Be genuine in what you say.

Don't embarrass the person. Let the message be one that can be received privately—even "covertly."

Send a message that you know will bring a smile to the other person's face. Smiles and encouragement go together!

4 ◆ Send Flowers or a Gift of Beauty

A gift of beauty conveys to another person, "You deserve beauty. You deserve recognition. You get both from me." In that, there's great encouragement to someone feeling down, overextended, or underappreciated.

The bouquet of flowers you send need not be an elaborate one. A single stem or a small nosegay can convey just as much meaning as a flowering tree.

Incentive Sometimes the "container" might be the more valuable or beautiful gift. Consider sending a single flower in a beautiful crystal vase with a note saying the rest of the flowers will arrive when the project is completed. Then, as promised, send a bundle of flowers later on, sans container.

Signature You may want to develop a "signature flower." Perhaps a yellow rose or a bunch of white daisies or a pot of pink hyacinth always says "you" to another person. If a particular flower is significant to you and someone else, give sprigs of that flower to each other to mark happy moments. No notes required!

(Remember: men like flowers, too.)

Other Gifts of Beauty The gift of beauty should not be limited to flowers. Send a friend a piece of driftwood with the note, "Life has a way of wearing us down into something beautiful." Or send a beautiful oversized postcard with a scene from one of our national parks, with the note, "Wish you were there. . . . Wish I could go, too. . . . Maybe someday. . . . Maybe when you finish your current project!"

The gift of beauty may be a poster, an illustration, or a child's work of art. It might be a paperweight, a sun catcher, or a seashell.

Be sure to include a message from the heart. Point out that ALL of God's creation has beauty—including the person who is receiving your gift. You might say, "As far as I'm concerned, you're a wonderful part of God's beautiful creation!"

The person who is anxious, depressed, or discouraged often loses sight of all that is beautiful in this world. Help restore that sensitivity!

5 ♦ Be Present in the Crisis

Just "being there" can provide great encouragement, especially in moments of crisis.

Is someone you know facing a difficult moment, an emotionally demanding situation, or a major life transition . . .

- at the hospital—or the outpatient clinic?
- at the funeral home?
- at the bankruptcy auction?
- at the divorce court?

Be There Nothing will mean quite as much as your physical presence.

Is the moving van about to pull away?

Does the office need to be cleared in the wake of a pink slip or "reduction in staff" notice?

Is a child flying away to college from a gate at your local airport?

Is the locker room quiet after the loss of the most important game of the season?

Show up.

Be Sensitive You don't need to say a great deal, if anything. Just "be there." Following a loved one's

death, the most appropriate message may be saying
only, "I'm sorry. I love you. And that's all I called to
say right now. I'll see you at the funeral." The grieving person won't need to respond or talk or explain
or be strong.

Don't feel as if you need to make small talk. Don't
trivialize the moment. Don't offer bright, cheery
comments as if nothing has happened. Sometimes
the most encouraging act is just to hunker down in
the gloom with someone and share the sadness.

Be Practical If your relationship with the person
is such that it's appropriate, offer to help out in a
practical way during the crisis. Load boxes. Carry
equipment. Fix a meal. Run an errand. Ask, "Is there
something I can do with these two hands and two
feet to help you right now? Can I get anything for
you, make any calls on your behalf, or pick up or
deliver anything or anybody?"

You might offer to baby-sit children or pick up a
relative at the airport. Perhaps the person would like
for you to come along to help recall later precisely
what the doctor says.

Being there says that your care and affection for
the person override your personal schedule or
agenda. It says that you consider the person to be
more important than any task or project. Very few
deeds can be more encouraging than that!

6 ◆ Award an Appropriate "Trophy"

Every child looks for the prize at the bottom of the box. We adults often have too many boxes without prizes. Take time and make the effort to "reward" someone who is feeling unrewarded.

Engraved Awards For a friend attempting to quit smoking, present a small trophy that says: "Winner. Thirty Smoke-Free Days."

To a young mother, hand a certificate that reads: "Congratulations! You have survived 2,832 days of motherhood without a nervous breakdown!" (Be as precise as possible with your count of days!)

To a special friend, give a small plaque that reads: "A Friend Who Always Seems to Be There When It Counts the Most."

Verbal Awards Your challenge is to ferret out unheralded accomplishments and blow a trumpet or two.

Perhaps the person has fed the dog faithfully day in and day out for years. Do you appreciate that fact? Even more important, do you appreciate the steadfastness of character in such a person? Say so!

Perhaps your wife has changed more diapers than

she can count—a thankless job if there ever was one. Do you appreciate her willingness to be an at-home mother? Have you let her know recently that you count her role in your family to be just as important as yours? Let her know!

Perhaps your husband has been employed every day of your twenty-three years of marriage and has never missed a mortgage payment on the home you both share. Have you thanked him lately? Express your appreciation.

Such "trophies"—small tributes to life's daily challenges—keep us from taking people for granted, even as they help other people feel more appreciated and encouraged. They call attention to the accomplishments earned through faithful, steadfast discipline. They uncover good attributes and call attention to successes rather than failures.

Friendly trophies say, "I noticed." In a world where so much good goes unnoticed, the fact that someone did is encouraging.

7 ◆ Invite the Person to Come Along

Nobody likes to feel left out. Nobody likes to feel like a fifth wheel.

And yet, that's how many people feel in the wake of a relationship loss—be it spouse, fiancée, or any other significant, serious, or long-term relationship. They have a sense of being isolated, rejected, alone. The only thing that truly helps is to be with other people.

Not for Couples Only Invite the "alone" person to the party. Take him to the game, to the mall, or to a special restaurant. Let her know that you consider her to be a person who is interesting and worthy to be around.

The same goes for those who are flying solo—who may not be in a relationship or who may have been out of a relationship for some time. Include them in the group.

You may have to put up with some tears. You may need to listen to some sad stories. That's part of being a friend.

Very often in cases of divorce, the friends of the couple tend to become divided into camps of "his friends" and "her friends." The worst scenario, how-

ever, is for the divorcing person to have "no friends."
You may need to let both parties know that you have
no intention of taking sides, except that you want to
be "by their side" and to support each one emotionally, socially, and spiritually in any way you can.

Keep in mind that . . .

- not all dinner parties need to have an even number of chairs around the table.
- not all events need to be "couples only."
- not all outings need to have an equal number of
  men and women.

Help in Trying Times Sometimes the loss is
not that of a person but that of a job or a business.
Don't exclude from your usual social gatherings the
person who is recently unemployed or who is experiencing a business failure. Both need your friendship
more than ever.

Sometimes the loss is that of a child from the
home (perhaps to college or a job, perhaps to death,
perhaps through loss of custody). Don't be shy about
including that person or couple in your family activities.

Very often, people do not include those who are
experiencing a difficult time—a discouraging event
or a depressing circumstance—because they don't
want to "hurt" them further, or they don't know what
to say to them. Your lack of an invitation will hurt
more than if you extend one; the invited person can
always decline if he chooses or leave early if he finds
the experience painful. As for what to say—ask the

person if there are topics she'd rather not discuss. Otherwise, be yourself and let the conversation flow freely.

The very fact that you invited the "alone" person to be a part of the group will be encouraging to him or her. It will help him or her regain a sense of identity and develop the ability to be alone without being lonely.

8 ♦ Show Up for the Big Event

Is your son about to make his stage debut?

Is your daughter about to take the field as part of the starting lineup?

Is your spouse about to be rewarded for community service?

Is your colleague about to finish that graduate degree—at last?

Is your neighbor about to be honored with a retirement party?

Are your aunt and uncle about to commemorate a fiftieth wedding anniversary?

Life has innumerable "big events" that loom large in the eyes of those being honored, feted, or spotlighted, and they deserve attention.

Do You Remember? Do you remember how you felt the day you gave your first piano recital? What would have been encouraging to you?

Do you remember the first time you took the floor in your basketball uniform—perhaps the first time in your life you had been in front of so many people? What would have helped you feel good about yourself in that moment?

Do you know what it feels like to be rewarded by

your colleagues . . . recognized by your peers . . . applauded by your supervisors . . . honored by your employees or those you lead?

Then you'll know that the one thing that means the most is for the people you love to be there, smiles on their faces, a "way to go, I'm proud of you" look in their eyes, and an attitude of "I'm for you" in the way they hold their shoulders back and their heads high.

Go the Extra Mile   Children often don't remember whether they won or lost the game or whether they hit all the right notes. They remember who was there for them. The same is true for adults. Being there says you care.

- For some, attendance at life's "big events" means juggling an impossible schedule.
- For some, it means racing to catch the last plane home.
- For some, it means canceling a standing appointment or missing a meeting.
- For some, it means donning a dreaded tux and forgoing a Monday night football game to listen to a dull speaker and eat overcooked green beans.

It always means putting the other person's joy ahead of your own desires. And that's what makes your "showing up" so encouraging. It's really an act of unselfish love.

9 ♦ Stop Doing the Harmful Thing

A number of us are agents of discouragement. We usually don't mean to be. As human beings, we simply make mistakes, do what's irritating, cause hurt, or disappoint. And when our mistakes, irritable qualities, painful jabs, and disappointing acts become habitual—like it or not—we cause discouragement. Sometimes, we cause it in those we love the most, and that makes facing up to our actions all the more painful.

Reversing the Trend Here are six steps that you might consider for reversing the trend from discouragement to encouragement.

1. *Find out what you are doing that is causing the other person to become discouraged.* The causes can usually be determined by asking one or more of these questions:

- *"What do I do that you wish I would quit doing?"*
- *"What do I do that irritates you the most?"*
- *"If you could change one thing about my behavior, what would it be?"*

2. *Look for the root cause.* If your wife says, "I wish you would quit throwing your socks on the floor," you might probe the comment (if you are brave enough to do so) and discover that not only are you a slob, but your careless lack of regard for housework makes your wife feel as if you expect her to be your housecleaning slave. If your husband says, "I wish you would quit banging around in the kitchen and vacuuming the house while I'm trying to watch the game," you might uncover a deeper truth. He resents what he perceives to be your attempts at distracting him from a pleasurable activity.

3. *Determine a level at which you are willing to make concessions in behavior.* Are you willing to pick up your socks? Are you willing to show more appreciation for the work your spouse does around the house? Are you willing to help with the housework?

You may need to negotiate. Life is full of negotiation and power sharing. Be wary if one person always seems to come out "on top" or be dominant in a series of confrontations. An explosion may lie in your future!

At times, you may encounter points beyond which you cannot bend. Express them and see what you can do to work around them. At still other times, you may need to back away from the present problem and define a better future. If you reach an impasse, get professional help.

4. *Apologize for the deeper hurt.* Express your sorrow for having caused a misunderstanding or hurt feelings or displaying a lack of appreciation. Ask forgiveness.

5. *Ask for help as you attempt to make the changes in the future.* Ask for patience. Solicit helpful advice.

6. *Make an appointment for discussing the issue again.* Put it on your calendar. Make a date several weeks away. That will allow time for wounds to heal and emotions to cool, time to make changes or at least show good faith in attempting to make changes.

Simply showing a willingness to face habits that discourage and a desire to change them is encouraging! It's even more encouraging when those changes occur and relationships grow as a result of enhanced communication and greater expressions of caring.

10 ◆ Lend a Listening Ear

Many people are seeking someone who will listen to their problems. Generally speaking, discouraged, depressed, or disappointed persons need to talk. They need the opportunity to vent their pain, to give voice to their anger, to express their sorrow, to confess their faults, to give words to their feelings.

Don't be too quick to empathize or to say, "I know just how you feel." In the first place, you don't know exactly how they feel. Pain is extremely individualized. In the second place, although the person needs to know that he is experiencing normal human emotions and that he hasn't fallen victim to a unique isolated circumstance, he also needs the opportunity to express his feelings without interruption.

Focus Your Attention Listening requires effort. It takes concentration, focus, and the ability to look a person in the eye and really "hear with the heart" the words being spoken. Don't allow people, things, or activity around you to distract you from listening intently.

In such conversations, strive to listen at least twice as much as you talk. (After all, you have two ears and only one mouth.)

Ask Questions Ask questions or make statements that invite conversation and that are difficult to dismiss with "yep" or "nope" answers, such as:

- *"That sounds like a great story. Tell it to me!"*
- *"Have you ever had an experience like this before?"*
- *"How does this make you feel?"*
- *"Given the circumstances, what do you think is likely to happen?"*
- *"How do you picture your ideal world?"*
- *"What would you like to be doing five years from now?"*
- *"What is it that you really enjoy doing for fun?"*
- *"What are you doing to change things?"*

This last question is critical in avoiding a codependent relationship. The codependent person tends to respond to a crisis, "What can I do about this for you?" In other words, "How can I shield you from this pain or change the circumstances for you or fight your battle?" The healthy relationship is based on the question: "What are you going to do about your life—your past, present, future? What can I do to help you accomplish your goals?"

Jesus Christ frequently asked those He helped: "What is it that *you* want?" The New Testament never portrays Him as imposing His will upon persons capable of exerting their own. He is recorded as saying more than once, "I don't condemn you; *you* go now and sin no more," implying, "It's within your capacity to do so." He also said to those who were helped,

"Your faith in Me has made you whole," implying, "Not My faith in you."

Having a listening ear is perhaps the foremost way to draw out of another person the answers that are right for him or her. Give the discouraged person the opportunity to voice his discouragement. In so doing, he may well find answers . . . and in that, encouragement.

11 ◆ Give or Share a Tape

A discouraged person often spins a virtually airtight cocoon around himself as a defensive move against the possibility of experiencing even more pain and disappointment. Generally, this withdrawal stage is the first stage of a healing process; it rarely lasts forever.

Don't be surprised if a discouraged person pushes away your friendship or withdraws from you. Chances are, she's withdrawing from everybody and everything she has known to regain a sense of personal identity and balance.

That doesn't mean you should give up and walk away. Eventually the wounded person needs to be drawn out and restored. She needs to face all areas of her life again in order to sift and sort and to put pieces back together in new and creative ways.

How Can You Help? First, allow the person to have a little space. Back off and let the person breathe.

Second, try giving the person a tape. Choose a tape that says what you would like to say to the person or that conveys a hopeful sentiment.

- It may be a music tape.
- It may be an inspirational series of tapes.
- It may be audio or video.

Inspire   Choose something uplifting. Choose humor. If you know the type of music that the person enjoys, choose something of that genre.

Perhaps you could tape a complete evening prayer service. Or you could record various cuts from albums you know the person enjoys.

Add a note with the tape you give: "I enjoyed this. Thought you might, too." Or "This artist really captured some of the ways I have felt in his music." Or "This is one of my top five movies of all time. Hope you enjoy it, too."

Reach Out   A tape lays a foundation for a future conversation, giving you and your discouraged friend or colleague something to talk about other than past problems.

Also, a tape requires little effort to consume. Discouraged or anxious people often have a problem concentrating; reading is often difficult.

The gift of a tape sends a message, "I'm still here. I'm not giving up on you."

12 ♦ Admit You Were Wrong

Oh, how stubborn many of us are in maintaining our position—even when we suspect we may be wrong! Such stubbornness can be wounding to others. Over time, the person who is continually told his ideas have no merit, his decisions are wrong, or his opinions are invalid will become discouraged. The same is true for the individual who loses every argument or who never hears an admission of "I was wrong, you were right" from another person.

To become an encourager rather than a discourager . . .

Point Out the Merit of Certain Ideas Give applause when it's deserved. (You won't be a lesser person for it but a greater one!)

Admit Your Mistakes Don't try to justify why you did certain things, thought a certain way, or drew certain conclusions. Just admit that you were wrong. Learn to say, "I'm sorry. I was wrong on that one." Thank the person for showing you the right way.

Acknowledge Good Outcomes   Perhaps you did not agree initially with a decision or course of action. Say, "I can see now why you did that." Or "I can see the benefits of having chosen this course."

Eliminate "I told you so" from your lexicon   If a mistake has obviously terrible repercussions, talk to the person in these terms, "I've been thinking about how we might improve this situation. Here are three of my ideas for your consideration." (By providing alternatives, you aren't setting yourself up as having the "right" way with all other ways labeled "wrong." You are giving the decision maker options.)

Recognize That All Opinions Have Merit
Each person has the right, privilege, and responsibility of his or her own ideas. The ideas may not be appropriate for a particular group of people, at a particular time, or in a particular circumstance. They may not be feasible or workable. They may not be affordable. But . . . they are not stupid, dumb, or worthless. All ideas and opinions have within them the potential to lead to new and better ideas and opinions. The most off-the-wall ideas frequently trigger a creative chain reaction resulting in a truly ingenious solution to a problem.

In recognizing another person's ideas, decisions, and opinions as having merit, you'll be affirming the value of the person and encouraging a continued flow of communication and creativity.

13 ♦ "Sit a Spell"

Beyond "showing up" is "sticking around."

Sometimes it's good to just sit awhile with the person who is wounded, grieving, anxious, or in pain. To such a person you are giving the highly valuable gifts of time and attention. Both are encouraging.

The Agenda Let the other person talk. Allow the person to be silent, too. "Sitting a spell" allows the wounded person to set the agenda. Your role is to be quietly present, available when needed, attentive when required, a silent sentinel against loneliness.

You might take along something to do with your hands, especially if it doesn't preclude your ability to listen. You might be able to knit, embroider, do needlepoint, tie a fishing lure, or whittle a bar of soap.

Mealtimes You might "sit a spell" while sharing a meal. Perhaps each can bring a sack lunch or pick up something from the deli and then swap portions. Mealtimes are often the loneliest parts of the day for a person who has recently lost a loved one to divorce or death.

Appointments "Sitting a spell" might also mean going with the person to a doctor's or dentist's appointment and sitting in the waiting room.

Play "Sitting a spell" might mean holding down one end of the sofa while you both watch television or a video.

Just sit on the front porch and watch a child play in the yard. The child can talk to you as he wills. Your presence makes you accessible but not stifling. That's the best position for "sitting a spell"—be available but not oppressively so.

Your presence wards off the feelings of isolation that can be so overwhelming to the distraught or discouraged person—far more so than anything you say or do. And there's really no substitute for it.

14 ♦ Seek Out the Lonely

Discouraged people are often in hiding because of a purposeful decision or their circumstances. You need to seek them out!

Where Are the Lonely? Consider the nursing homes. Do you have a friend who has recently moved into a nursing home or convalescent hospital? Have you visited him or her lately? Stop by!

Consider the retirement centers. Would someone you know appreciate a friendly visit? Plan a time to get together.

Consider those who may be homebound. Perhaps they are no longer able to drive, or they may have become the primary caregivers of an ailing spouse or friend. What can you do to brighten their day?

Consider the person who may be recently home from a hospital stay—perhaps recovering from an injury or suffering with a long-term or terminal illness. Your visit would mean a great deal!

Consider, too, the person who may be in prison. What can you do to encourage the person to live a positive life in a negative environment? What might you do to help him or her prepare for a productive life after parole?

Friendly Presence   After the initial shock of an illness, death, or divorce—and the resulting initial rush of concerned friends to his side—the wounded person often finds himself feeling somewhat abandoned, especially if the recovery process is delayed or long-term. This is your opportunity to be a friendly oasis in a lonely desert.

You may want to take along a plate of cookies, a pie, or a cake. You may want to pick up a couple of sandwiches and share a "lunch hour" with the person. (If you suspect that the person may be on a specialized diet, check in advance about any dietary restrictions.)

You may want to take along a book, videotape, or other item to leave with the person, preferably something that doesn't have to be returned.

Sparkling Conversation   You need not take anything, however, for your visit to be meaningful. Just a few minutes of conversation with someone from the "outside world" can be a great blessing to the person who feels confined.

Focus your conversations outward. Tell about what you are doing. Discuss current events. Share news about mutual friends. Help the person to feel connected with the world outside her four walls.

Special Ideas   You may want to take church bulletins to homebound members of your church and share news of the congregation.

Perhaps a friend has been in a serious accident and has become disabled. Drop by on a regular basis to discuss current affairs and the latest books and movies. (With the aid of television, newspapers and magazines, a videocassette player, and a books-on-wheels library program to supply audiocassette versions of books, your friend can keep up-to-date.) Limited physical mobility doesn't keep his mind from being alive with ideas, opinions, and questions.

A frail senior citizen may enjoy a ride around town occasionally. Urge her to point out the places of historic interest, recall stories about the local people, and share what it was like to be living there in a different era.

The encouragement you give to the lonely is invariably returned to you many times over. As is true in so many areas of life, the giver receives more than he gives.

15 ◆ The Letter of Appreciation

The law of entropy—the law by which things grind to a halt unless they receive new bursts of energy—seems to operate in relationships as well as in the physical world! Relationships tend to stagnate or die unless they are renewed. One of the best ways to renew a relationship is to express appreciation for it.

It takes less than five minutes to write several sentences of heartfelt appreciation. Your letter, however, can provide a month's worth of satisfaction to those who help you make it through life.

To People at Work Write your boss or your coworkers a letter: "I've just been thinking over our past (X number of) years together, and I want to tell you how much they've meant to me. I appreciate the work you do. I appreciate the ways in which you've challenged me and caused me to grow as a person." Be specific in what you write. Let the person know that his or her life has made a difference.

To People at Home Write your spouse a love letter. (When was the last time you did?) Tell her why you'd marry her all over again. Point out specific ways in which you feel you've grown and developed as a person because of your marriage.

Write a love letter to your children. Let them know that you're glad they were born and how blessed you feel to be their parent.

To People in the Community Write a letter of applause to your pastor who deals mostly with problems. What a wonderful respite to get a positive stroke of appreciation. The same goes for your local politicians and community leaders. Most of their work involves problems and crises. How encouraging for them to hear a good word!

Consider your family physician. Drop a note: "I'm not sick. I realized recently that I see you only when I'm not truly myself. Well . . . today I am definitely in sound mind and body, and I wanted to say, 'Thank you for taking care of me and my family all these years.' "

Don't overlook your child's teacher. Or your favorite clerk at your favorite department store. Or the teller at the bank who has treated you with courtesy and professionalism. Or the postal carrier who has been on the beat in your neighborhood for as long as you can remember. Don't forget the local police department or fire station—where your note of thanks and appreciation is almost sure to make the staff bulletin board!

16 ◆ The Unexpected Letter of Commendation

We sometimes overlook the fact that our bosses have bosses . . . our children's teachers have principals . . . our pastors have district superintendents or bishops.

Consider writing a letter of commendation about those whose quality of work and faithfulness you appreciate. Don't send it to the person but to the one for whom the person works or the one to whom the person reports.

Let your boss's boss know the things you appreciate about your boss. Point out his or her fine qualities as a person and as a supervisor. Managers frequently are appraised from the "top down"—rarely is the picture complete from that vantage point. Let your boss's boss in on some of the good things your boss does that go unrecognized.

Let your pastor's supervisor know how much you appreciate your pastor's sermons or her cool head and warm heart in times of crisis or his compassion for the hurting people in your congregation.

Let the principal at your child's school know how much you appreciate your child's teacher . . . and why.

Let your best employees' families know just how

well their family member is doing or how much the work is appreciated. Your letter of applause will raise your employee's status at home and may make it easier to justify the intense effort your employee gives to the job.

A letter of commendation encourages every person who reads it.

Write from a Neutral "Political Position"
Don't write a letter to sway opinion in a showdown circumstance. Write when the status quo is holding.

Write a Letter Appropriate for the Time Frame
Don't gush over your pastor's great preaching ability if you've heard him preach only one sermon. Don't rave about your child's teacher the second week of class. Rather . . . write about your boss as you mark your own five-year anniversary or after a major project has been completed successfully. Write a note about your child's teacher after the school term ends. Write a note to your pastor after he's been there at least a year (during which time you've attended faithfully!).

Write Only the Positive
Don't use compliments to introduce grievances.

Write Briefly
You may say simply, "Sometimes top-level executives don't always know what fine people they have working for them. I want to let you know that, as far as I'm concerned, you have a real winner in Lynn Doe. These are three things I espe-

cially appreciate about my boss, traits and accomplishments about which you may not know . . ." Then list the points and conclude, "As of this week, I've been with this company for X number of years, and one of the main reasons I continue to enjoy coming to work on Monday mornings is Lynn Doe."

17 ◆ Provide a Helping Hand

We all dig ourselves into holes at times. When that happens, we attempt to scramble our way up the slippery sides of the hole by ourselves—often falling repeatedly and perhaps even injuring ourselves along the way—or we sit down and give up. The better alternative is to cry for help.

As encouragers, we need to be alert for the person who is in a way-over-his-head predicament and isn't calling for help.

In being an encourager . . .

Quietly Move Alongside to Help   Don't attempt to call the shots or take control over the situation. Ask what you can do, where you can fit into the project, and then follow through.

Be Prepared for the Mundane   The nitty-gritty chores are often the most needed.

Don't Be a Prima Donna   Even if your forte is decorating, the need may be for a dishwasher. Be prepared to assist where you are most needed, not where you are most qualified.

Arrive Ready to Work   Many tasks can be done with conversation. Others can't. You may find yourself working in isolation. Be prepared to do whatever it takes.

Don't Expect Lavish Praise or Thanks
The person overwhelmed by a project may be so mentally harried or physically exhausted that he or she can't comprehend all that you've done.

Nothing encourages a person carrying a heavy load as much as having someone come along to help shoulder it.

18 ♦ Forgive the Debt

Debt must surely be one of the top-ten discouragers of all time. It has destroyed countless relationships through the ages, wreaked havoc in families and societies, and caused innumerable suicides and premature deaths through stress. The Holy Bible refers to debt as a "curse." Anybody who struggles under its weight knows that to be true.

Does someone owe you money?

Is it an honest debt, truly based on the person's need or extenuating circumstances?

Must you be repaid to stay out of debt yourself?

If your answers are yes, yes, and no . . . consider canceling the debt. You'll provide an enormous amount of encouragement to your debtor.

Courses of Action In forgiving a debt . . .

- put your desire to cancel the debt in writing.

Let the person have more than just your spoken word of forgiveness. Such a document will establish the fact of the debt and assure the person that you are sincere in your forgiving the amount owed.

- don't replace one type of debt for another.

Don't have a hidden agenda or attach strings to your offer. For example, "I'd like to cancel your debt, and I'm hoping that you'll hire my nephew in your firm." Or "Let's forget the amount you owe me; I hope I can count on your endorsement." These aren't true debt cancellations. You're simply requiring a different sort of payback.

Special Circumstances The debt owed you may not be money. It may be a debt of the "I owe you one" variety—a favor or gift of time or service. Be sensitive to the fact that people often volunteer their services and time only to be overcome by circumstances that keep them from fulfilling their commitment. Let someone off the hook if you know in your heart that it's the best thing to do for the person.

At other times, you may want to offer a person an easier way of paying a debt—such as smaller payments over a longer period of time, canceling the interest portion of a loan payback, or accepting a payout in work rather than cash.

You might not be able to cancel an entire debt, but you might be able to reduce the amount owed. For example, request out-of-pocket expenses and cancel the payment owing for your labor.

You may be in a position to cancel a debt with this stipulation: "Provide for me proof of your having gone to a credit counselor or a certified financial advisor and your debt with me will be marked paid in full." For someone who is careless with money and has a harmful pattern of overspending and overextending, this payback in training can be long-term encouragement.

Canceling a loan should *not* be done if it will encourage laziness, slothfulness, or greed in another person. Such a loan cancellation doesn't really encourage; it enables the person to maintain an unhealthy, irresponsible pattern of borrowing and spending.

On the other hand, canceling a loan when the amount clearly represents the presence of need or an honest mistake can greatly encourage a person to move forward with head held high!

19 ◆ Provide Material or Financial Assistance

Encouragement of this kind comes in many forms:

- To the hungry person, encouragement comes in the form of a loaf of bread.
- To the person without proper clothing in winter, encouragement comes in the form of a warm coat and new shoes.
- To the person without the means to make a house payment, encouragement comes in the form of a house payment.
- To the person without transportation, encouragement comes in the form of bus tokens or a new alternator for the old car.

Anonymous Gifts In nearly all cases, the best method for material and financial assistance is the "anonymous gift." The basket of fruit and vegetables that shows up on the porch. The envelope with cash that's slid under the door (or the money order that arrives in the mail). The sack of clothing delivered by a "hired messenger" (with all items clean and in good repair). The box of school supplies brought to the door.

Items that you give to others need not be new or

expensive. Vegetables and fruit might come from your garden and orchard. The clothes may be those of a family member who has outgrown them. The point is not to provide the best, newest, or showiest but to meet a real need with as much quality as possible.

Who Needs Help? Sometimes the person needing material or financial assistance is not the one who has nothing (for example, the person out of a job or unable to work at the present time), but the person barely making it.

To the single parent struggling to work and raise her two small children, encouragement comes in the form of a trusted friend picking up the children for an evening so she can have the house, the TV, and the bathtub all to herself.

To the young couple with hardly a dollar left over at the end of the month, encouragement comes in the form of a gift certificate for dinner and a movie.

To the elderly man on a fixed income, encouragement comes in the form of someone arriving in the spring to pull weeds and returning in the fall to rake leaves.

To the wife and mother recently home from the hospital, encouragement comes in the form of a couple of casserole dishes and a friend who can push a vacuum cleaner.

Encouragement is finding the area of need in a person's life and doing your best to fill it.

20 ◆ Let Go

Having someone cling to you too tightly or too long is discouraging.

Conversely, having someone let you go—allowing you more space, more freedom, more choices, more mobility than you previously had—can be tremendously encouraging.

If you are holding someone back, for whatever the reason, consider letting go. Allow the person to take the reins . . . to fly solo . . . to try the new thing . . . to explore.

Who Are You Holding Back? We often hold back our children from participating in certain activities because we are afraid they will get hurt. We must recognize that holding them back can also be a source of pain to them! Appraise the situation as honestly as you can. Seek the advice of professionals. Talk to other parents who have been through what you're facing. And as much as possible, let go.

This certainly is not to advocate that you allow a child to do whatever he or she pleases or to permit any activity within your home that is illegal or immoral. It is not to say that you should sanction immoral or illegal behavior outside your home! It is to say that the time inevitably comes when a child is best served by letting him ride his bicycle without the training wheels—even if it means a few crashes and scraped knees. The time comes when a child needs to leave home—even if you can no longer know with certainty where she is and what she may be doing at 2:00 A.M.

Sometimes we hold back our colleagues and friends because we are afraid of losing their friendship or afraid that in their success, they will forget about us. Let go. You'll kill your friendship or working relationship by holding on too tightly.

Sometimes we hold back our spouses because we are afraid of losing authority over them or intimacy with them. The result of holding back tends to be resentment and anger—both of which will cause a person eventually to flee!

Discuss the Situation How do you know if you are holding others back? They'll probably tell you so. "Don't worry so much," they might say. Or "You don't own me." Or "You're smothering me." Or "I've got to be me." If you hear such statements, engage in an honest, straightforward discussion: "Please tell me exactly what you'd like to be doing and how I'm holding you back." Be prepared for a blunt conversation.

Let the person know about your concerns. If the issue is rooted in morality, voice your opinions. If the issue involves the law, state the consequences. Raise every caution sign you want, but when all is said, let go. In some cases, you may be able to negotiate a compromise (which is an excellent way for you to build trust even as your loved one tries his wings).

The tendency to cling to others is often rooted in fear. Fear discourages.

Have faith in people. Trust them to give life their best effort. Believe in their ability to achieve success. Faith encourages.

21 ♦ Provide an Animal to Pet

During the past decade, amazing discoveries have been made in hospitals, nursing homes, rehabilitation centers, and retirement communities across our nation. The conclusion is that pets can aid the healing process.

Therapeutic Value Pets seem to be valuable in many ways.

1. The isolated, discouraged, ill, or lonely person is put in touch—literally—with something alive, whole, warm, and vibrant. Touching, stroking, holding, cuddling, and playing with a living creature—especially a dog or cat—encourage living!

2. The depressed or despondent person tends to display an increased will to live when animals are around. A sense of responsibility for a living creature seems to go hand in hand with a desire to live.

3. The person who is feeling unloved, rejected, or abandoned benefits from contact with an animal that displays unconditional love and loyalty—even through the wagging of a puppy's tail or the mewing of a sleepy kitten.

4. The person with high blood pressure and rapid

heartbeat actually tends to experience a lowering of blood pressure and heart rate while stroking a pet.

5. The person who is uncommunicative, angry, or frustrated often benefits from having a pet with an unbiased opinion, a listening ear, and no argumentative opinions! There's an advantage perceived in talking aloud to a pet—giving voice to concerns and hurts—even if the pet can't talk back!

Guidelines Want to encourage a discouraged person? Take along your pet for him to hold or play with.

Want to encourage a friend who has recently lost a spouse to death or divorce? Consider buying her a pet. But discuss the purchase with her first.

Not all animals are for all people, however. Follow some commonsense guidelines:

- Only take your animal along if it is, indeed, a friendly animal with good "pet-ability." No aloof cats or sulking dogs, please! Kittens and puppies are generally easier to hold and cuddle than are full-grown cats and dogs.
- Don't take an animal to which your friend might be allergic. Ask in advance.
- Don't allow your animal to run wild in the person's room, home, or neighborhood.
- Before buying a housepet for a friend, consider the living arrangements. Is it an apartment? Does the apartment manager allow animals? What is the work schedule? Does she travel a great deal? Does he work nights? Is she an out-

doorsy person? Is he the indoor type? Try to find a pet that would be a good match for your friend's temperament and life-style. For example, you may find that fish are the most relaxing pets you can find for your high-stress, high-tech colleague. On the other hand, a big dog with whom to jog in the mornings may be the best pet for your lonely suburban friend.

- Don't take an animal to a person who is afraid of that type of animal (be it bird or bird dog). Don't assume that your pet will help that person overcome a lifelong fear.
- Check with a nursing home or hospital before taking a pet onto its premises.

22 ♦ Accentuate the Positive

It might be the miracle story in your own life.

It might be a story you read in a magazine or heard on a television program.

It might be an incident in the life of a friend or loved one.

Whatever the story, if it's a positive one with merit and applicability to the discouraged person, tell it! Keep the good news flowing.

The New Testament of the Bible offers this advice:

> Whatever things are true,
> Whatever things are noble,
> Whatever things are just,
> Whatever things are pure,
> Whatever things are lovely,
> Whatever things are of good report,
> If there is any virtue and
> If there is anything praiseworthy—
>   meditate on these things.
> —Philippians 4:8

Certainly those beautiful words are appropriate for any person in any era. What is truly amazing, however, is that they are the words of a man, the apostle

Paul, who by his own account endured five floggings (of thirty-nine lashes each); three beatings with rods; one stoning; three shipwrecks; a day and a night floundering in the open sea; seemingly endless journeys, weariness, hunger, thirst, fastings, exposure to the environment; and virtually constant criticism from all sides during the last half of his life. The words written to the Philippians came from the quill of a man imprisoned (and in retrospect, living on "death row")!

Hold Out Hope Rather than tell your discouraged friend about the time you felt just as down, tell him what you did to get "up" again.

Rather than tell your sick friend about a relative who died of the same ailment, tell her about the person you know who survived the disease and has gone on to live a full and meaningful life.

Rather than console your divorcing friend with statistics that put him in the majority of his age group in our society, tell him about how your broken heart was healed, and encourage him to look to the future with hope.

Rather than commiserate with your bankrupt friend over the national debt, explore concrete ideas about how she might regain her financial balance.

If there's a 60 percent chance of failure, focus on the 40 percent chance of success.

If there's a 90 percent prediction of death, focus on the 10 percent possibility of life.

For every negative prognosis or projection, there's at least one "exception." Choose to talk about it.

Believe the Best   You don't need to ignore reality or overlook difficulties, however. Face them with hope, believing for the best possible outcome and continuing to believe, no matter what circumstances arise.

Believe for the marriage to be healed until the divorce decree is final.

Believe for the disease to be cured or go into remission until the final breath.

Believe for the child to return home until she does.

And even when divorce, death, and disappointment prevail, keep believing for something good to come in the future. Every end is the beginning of something else.

The tragic story, the down-turned countenance, and the negative outlook discourage.

The uplifting story, the smiling face, and the forward-looking gaze encourage.

23 ◆ Be Loyal

When the going gets tough . . .

When criticism starts to fly . . .

When accusations are hurled . . .

Or when threats are issued against someone you know and love . . .

Stand up! Voice your support. Point out the person's positive traits, accomplishments, and actions. Exhibit your loyalty in terms that are clear.

In the aftermath of the attempted 1991 coup against Mikhail Gorbachev, former leader of the U.S.S.R., several of Gorbachev's aides were dismissed from their positions of power for exhibiting "passivity" in the face of the coup leaders' dictates. Feeling loyal didn't count; displaying loyalty did.

The Proper Defense Few of us will have colleagues, family members, friends, or superiors who face a major coup against them. Most of us, however, will have ample opportunity to defend those close to us against the gossip, lies, and slander we hear about them.

Often a simple comment of "I question that" or "I doubt that to be true" will suffice in squelching a harmful rumor. Sometimes it only takes saying,

"He's my friend" or "I don't know anything about that," to put a stop to an insidious plot.

In defending a friend . . .

- make sure you have correct information. Don't speculate. Get the facts as best you can. Go directly to your friend and ask if certain accusations hold water.
- make sure you have solid reasons for your supportive opinion. Know why you are on the side of your friend's decision, idea, vote, or course of action.

Outspoken Support   Even if your friend turns out to be the vilest criminal in recorded history (which is unlikely), you can stand by your friend and voice your support:

- *"I believe in my friend's potential. I know the good side of him. I choose to believe for good things in and from his life."*
- *"I acknowledge what my friend has done. I realize he is facing dire consequences. Still, that's all the more reason for me to be his friend now. If ever he needed a friend, he needs one now."*
- *"I know my friend has faults. So do we all. I choose to stand by him in his failure or weakness because I need other people to stand by me in mine."*

Your friendship need not be blind. It need only be strong.

Your loyal stance for your friend may be the only sign of encouragement he sees in an otherwise bleak situation. It may be the only cause for his not sinking into despair.

Loyalty calls you to put your reputation—and in some cases, even your job or life—on the line for another person. Can any act give greater encouragement or exhibit greater love?

24 ◆ Help the Person Get More Help

Few of us are trained as counselors or psychologists. Fewer still are psychiatrists with a medical understanding of the brain.

There comes a point when we must recognize that we are not able to provide all of the encouragement another person needs. When that point comes, we should consider the following actions:

Elicit Group Support Circle the wagons of your friends around the person. Provide an ongoing chain of encouragement. Get others involved in the process of providing assistance and support.

Suggest Training In some cases, a person needs information just as much or more than a shoulder to cry on. Formal study in communication, psychology, finance, nutrition, and so forth may provide the information your friend needs to "self-help" himself through the problem. In some cases, that training might come in a series of recommended books.

Suggest Professional Help Refer your friend to a licensed therapist—a qualified person adept in the particular area where your friend needs help. It may be

- a marriage counselor.
- a psychologist.
- a medical doctor.
- a financial planner.
- a loan officer.
- an attorney.
- a child-care expert.
- a consumer advocate.
- a police officer.
- a minister or priest.

In some cases, an intensive course of therapy may be warranted—perhaps admission to a hospital or clinic that provides inpatient treatment. Don't stigmatize that decision. Be grateful the person is willing to get help, and support the person in the decision to pursue prescribed treatment.

If the person is unwilling to seek professional help, you might suggest that both of you visit a trusted mutual friend (perhaps your priest or minister). Express your willingness to be told by the mutual party that you are overreacting or inappropriately concerned. Get a commitment from the other person to follow whatever advice is rendered.

Encourage Participation in a Support Group Literally millions of people have been helped through groups such as Alcoholics Anonymous, Weight Watchers, and countless other organizations that promote self-recovery and group accountability. Twelve-step programs are available today in nearly every area of human frailty and foible.

If the person refuses all suggestions or offers of additional help, you may need to confront the person with your inability to continue in the relationship as it presently exists. State your frustrations, weariness, and concerns in clear, simple, direct terms. Declare your intentions to get help for yourself and then do so.

Recognize the limits of your ability as an encourager. Do what you can. Ask others to help. And don't feel guilty for what you cannot do.

As your friend becomes more whole, he'll no doubt consider all of your actions as "encouraging" ones toward his health, even those that may have seemed painful or confrontational to him initially.

25 ♦ Commit to Friendship

No vows are necessary.
No formal declarations are required.
No outward and visible signs are warranted.

A Caring Commitment What is required for friendship? Commitment to go a second mile for another person.

- Listening, even when you want to talk.
- Crying together over things that matter to one of you.
- Being present in good times and bad times and lots of times in between.
- Sharing secrets, opinions, ideas, problems, jokes, and successes.
- Putting the other person's welfare before any task or event.
- Never being too busy to take a phone call.
- Remembering special days and marking special occasions in the other person's life.
- Celebrating the fact that the other person is alive on the earth.
- Always believing for the best and helping to overcome the worst.

Nothing is more encouraging than having a friend like that.

A Two-Way Commitment   It takes two, however, to have a friendship. You cannot simply decide to be someone else's friend. True friendship nearly always requires a mutuality of background, beliefs, and values.

A Determined Commitment   Furthermore, true friendship requires cultivation. It doesn't just happen overnight. It takes time . . . and more time. Encounters . . . and more encounters. Conversations . . . and more conversations. It requires a willingness to work through misunderstandings and survive differences of opinion, agreeing to disagree. It means overcoming jealousies and admitting weaknesses. Friendship takes effort.

And yet, perhaps nothing is more encouraging than knowing that you have a friend—a real, genuine, there-for-you, bona fide friend.

To have one, you need to be one.

In being one, you give the ultimate gift of encouragement to someone else.

26 ◆ Don't Give Up on the Person

Sometimes relationships flow smoothly; sometimes they don't. Sometimes we're in an upward spiral in which everything seems to be going our way; sometimes we can't find our way.

Steadfastness Perhaps the number one trait of the "encourager" is steadfastness. The encourager is the one who is there, believing all along that the discouraged person will get over it, will get through it, will get beyond it. The encourager is the one who rides out the storm, recognizing it as a storm and not the cataclysmic end of the world.

Let the person who is discouraged, despondent, or depressed know through your presence, your actions, and your words that you intend to be there to celebrate the end of the crisis. You intend to be present to greet the new dawn, to help reap the harvest of happiness, and to rejoice when the tide finally turns.

- Make contact regularly.
- Visit frequently.
- Call faithfully.

Choose to plod through the whole miserable experience and wade through each new swamp of problems, no matter how endless the journey may be.

Why? Only because you feel compelled to do so. Because you have chosen to do so. Because you are required by an inner impulse to do so.

The only reason to stop? If the other person wants you to stop or refuses to receive any encouragement you offer.

Persistence   You may not even like the person you are encouraging. The person may not be someone you consider a "friend." In fact, the person may not want your initial acts of kindness. Nevertheless, if there's something inside you that says, "You need to come through for this person," follow your instinct and do it—all the way to the end, expecting it to be a glorious one.

Life has a strange way of throwing us across the paths of others. Don't fight the fact that your boat crashed into a particular dock. Rejoice in it! However quirky events may seem, at another level they're likely to make sense and be part of a magnificent design too big for any of us to comprehend. Is there someone who seems to be set before you, someone who is willing to receive what you have to give, someone to whom you feel compelled to share your best and brightest rays of hope? Well . . . shine like the sun! And don't give up.

Things to Say

27 ♦ "I Really Like . . ."

Being an "encourager at large" is a little like being the Johnny Appleseed of compliments. Scatter words of approval wherever they are warranted. Speak them genuinely. Be generous in voicing good words. Don't say the same thing to everyone. Find new ways of expressing compliments.

Most people will hear twenty or more negative remarks for every positive one they hear. Choose to encourage with the positive comment.

You don't need to know a person to give a compliment about appearance. Sometimes the casual comment from the stranger in the elevator, the cabbie, the passing clerk, or the bellman really brightens a person's day.

Features Every person has at least one attractive physical feature. Take note of it.

- *"You've got a beautiful smile."*
- *"I really like your curly hair."*
- *"You have such graceful hands."*
- *"Your eyes are stunning."*
- *"I love the dimple that appears when you laugh."*

Apparel   At times, the object of your admiration might be something the person is wearing.

- *"That's a great-looking outfit."*
- *"I like your tie."*
- *"You really look great in that color."*

Bearing   At times, you can take note of the general way a person carries himself or projects his personality.

- *"You always come up with the most fabulous looks."*
- *"I like that hairstyle on you. You can carry it off when few people can."*
- *"You always enter a room looking so positive. I think it's the way you hold your shoulders back when you walk."*

The "New"   If you know someone who has embarked on a "new and improved look," make a positive comment.

- *"You're really looking great these days."*
- *"I like your new glasses."*
- *"Wow. Your nails look great today."*

The genuine compliment says to a person, "You're noteworthy. You're attractive." That's an encouraging news flash!

Your compliments will be appreciated in a special way just before a person is required to make an entrance or embark on a difficult task—for example, just prior to a sales presentation, the last thing before entering the boss's office, minutes before a first date, or the final seconds before the curtain goes up. Personal compliments about outward appearance often ignite the fires of inner confidence.

28 ♦ "Thank You"

Sometimes the simplest words of encouragement are "thank you."

Many a task goes unappreciated. Many a favor goes unrecognized. Many a noble deed remains unsung. All of which leads to discouragement.

Saying "thank you" tells a person . . .

- *"I appreciate what you have done."*
- *"You've made a positive difference."*
- *"What you did (or said or gave) has value (merit or importance)."*

The Thankless Task Lots of chores in life are routine and mundane. We even call them thankless tasks. What an encouragement to have someone thank you for doing them!

- *"Thanks for cooking such a good dinner."*
- *"Thanks for washing the car."*
- *"Thanks for taking out the trash this morning."*
- *"Thanks for mopping the floor."*

The Taken-for-Granted Performance We frequently overlook those who are closest and dearest to us. Have you thanked your parents lately for some of the things they've done for you through the years? Have you thanked your spouse for standing by you through thick and thin? Have you let your employees know how valuable they are to you? Stop for a moment and count all the things for which you have to be thankful. Start voicing those words of thanks to those who should hear them.

Think back over your childhood. Who played an important part in helping you become who you are today? A teacher? A neighbor? A Sunday school leader? A coach? Say "thank you" today. They'll be encouraged!

In Saying Thank You . . .

- Put your sentiments in writing whenever appropriate.
- Be specific. Cite a specific moment, gift, attribute, deed. Refer to time and place. Tell what you enjoyed or valued.
- Be timely. Don't wait until summer to write thank-you notes for gifts received in December!
- Be genuine. Don't overstate your case. Don't underplay your appreciation.

Saying "thank you" encourages a person to continue to do good by applauding what has already been done. It takes note of time, effort, and love. A heartfelt "thank you" touches the heart.

29 ♦ "You Really Did Well!"

Be generous in applauding the performance of others. They'll be encouraged!

What should you say? The direct, honest approach is the simplest and best.

- *"Congratulations on your award! You deserved to win!"*
- *"I really enjoyed your performance in (and name the theatrical, musical, or other on-stage production)."*

Tell the person how you felt.

- *"I was in stitches all night."*
- *"I was deeply moved."*
- *"You made me see the situation (or the composition) in a new light."*

Don't Overlook the Small Performance

Small accomplishments deserve praise, too. Let your staff at work know that you applaud their presentation made during the recent sales meeting. Compliment your friend on her team winning the bowling tournament. Let the teenager who mows your lawn hear you say, "You did a really great job!" as you hand him his payment.

Frequent Praise for Young People Children, especially, need to hear our applauding remarks on a frequent basis. The "performance" may be a piece of artwork from school or a good grade on a paper. "Great job!" Say it sincerely and if you have an ample supply of refrigerator magnets, post the good work for a day or two!

Children and teens need to know that you appreciate their effort, even if the team lost the game. They need to know that you appreciate their courage, even if they missed a word or two in reciting their lines. They need to know that you were watching with pride, even if they got out of step as the band marched down the street. Praise a child honestly for what he *has* done well rather than criticize what he has failed to do.

Pass Along a Press Clipping Has the local newspaper recently featured a photograph or article about a friend or an acquaintance? Cut it out and send it to your friend with a note: "Way to go! I thought you might like an extra copy of this, perhaps to send to a faraway friend or relative!"

Runner-Up Winners Don't overlook the person who comes in second, third or fourth. She is a winner, too!

30 ♦ "Here Is Something That Spoke to Me of You"

We frequently think of another person as we read the variety of messages that come our way or hear clever sayings or inspirational stories.

It may be a passage of poetry . . .

Or a verse of Scripture . . .

Or a bumper sticker . . .

Or a lighthearted story in the newspaper . . .

Or a slogan on a coffee mug found at a roadside cafe.

Messages Pass along the uplifting words! Let the person know that she was thought of in a good light and associated with a positive message. She'll be encouraged!

You don't need to buy the coffee mug or bumper sticker. Just pass along its message. Write out the words, and add a little note: "This reminded me of you."

If the words are something you can cut out (perhaps from a magazine or newspaper), do so. You can write in the margin next to the item, "Hope this brings a smile to your face. I thought of you when I read this."

Humor   Be cautious in sending jokes, cartoons, or funny stories. Don't send them unless you are 100 percent certain that you will be laughing with the person and not be perceived as laughing at him.

Special Interests   Be especially attuned to articles related to issues, projects, interests, hobbies, or careers of your friends—and especially so to items that appear in out-of-the-mainstream publications. Send the item with a brief note: "I found this interesting and wondered if you saw it. No need to return." The person will be encouraged that you were thinking about him, even if he already has the information. (Make certain the name and date of the publication are included in the clipping you send. The article may be one to reference or quote later.)

We all like to think that we rest pleasantly on the minds of other people. It's encouraging to have evidence that we do!

31 ♦ "What Can I Do to Help?"

These are perhaps the most welcome words that any person facing a task or crisis can hear: "What can I do to help you?" They are especially encouraging words if the person knows in what ways help is most needed. (The task or crisis might not be a big one; it might be facing the final five minutes before the turkey comes out of the oven!)

One person phrases it this way: "Here are ten fingers itching to be put to work. What can they do?"

"Would This Help?" At times, the offer of assistance may be better phrased, "Would this help?"—and then give a suggested way in which you are willing to help, able to help, or feel help might be important. The person who is sorely discouraged, depressed, or struggling with stress may not know what is needed. She may not be able to articulate where or in what ways she needs help. He may not be able to focus clearly enough to know his central problem! Offer some suggested ways.

- *"Would it help if we took the children for the weekend?"*
- *"Would it help you if I went with you?"*

- *"Would it help if I made this call for you?"*
- *"Wouldn't you like a little help in doing that? I'd certainly hate to have to do that alone."*

"I'd Like to . . ." At other times, a person may be reluctant to receive help or not know how to receive it or ask for it, even if it is needed and wanted. Try suggesting an act of assistance or comfort—"I'd like to do this for you. Is that O.K.?"

- *"I'd like to mow your yard. It's great exercise for me. Would it be all right with you if I did that?"*
- *"I'd like to bring over a container of soup I just made. Would that be O.K. with you?"*
- *"I'd like to drive you there. That way we could spend a little time together and you wouldn't need to worry about finding a parking place. O.K.?"*

Sensitive Sleuth Finding a way to help others requires only one thing: sensitivity. Become a "sleuth" (as opposed to a spy). Listen for your friend to express when he feels the most down, where she has trouble going, or who he is trying to avoid. Learn to recognize the "rough moments," and do what you can to ease them.

Consider this situation. A friend has spent many hours playing on the neighborhood tennis courts with her husband. Now that they are divorced, she is reluctant to return to the scene of happier times, even though she really enjoys playing tennis. Call her one Saturday morning and say, "Let's go play! It's time to make some new memories that are even better than the old ones!"

Helping hands express a loving heart. Both are encouraging.

32 ◆ "You Can Do This!"

The emphasis can be placed on each word in this encouraging statement.

"You *can do* this!" You have confidence in someone as a person of ability, talent, skill, courage, and fortitude. "You, as opposed to anyone else!" You might add, "Yes, *you!*"

When calling attention to the ability of a person, point out specific traits.

- *"You have the right temperament for this job."*
- *"You are uniquely qualified by your background for this task."*
- *"You have the strong convictions it takes for this position."*
- *"You have the right network of friends and associates to pull this off."*

"You can *do* this!" You have full confidence in the person's success. Not *might.* Not *maybe.* Not *have a chance.* But *can.*

Give reasons why you believe the person will succeed. Personality. Desire. Stick-to-it-iveness. Training. Contacts. Experience. Innate tendencies. Psy-

chological match. Giving reasons is like giving cleats
to a runner preparing to step into the starting blocks
of a project.

"You can do this!" You recognize the work
and effort that will be involved, and you believe the
person to be capable of success and willing to make
the effort it will take.

Sometimes people are discouraged because they
see too big a mountain of challenge ahead of them.
Rather than see the next day, they envision the next
forty years. Rather than imagine the next step in the
chain of events, they hurtle ahead in their imagina-
tions to a conclusion. Talk to the person in terms of
the next step: "Learn to crawl . . . and then you can
learn to walk . . . and then you can learn to run
. . . and then you can train for the dash or the mara-
thon." Break the task down to its component sub-
tasks: "You can pay off this credit card . . . and
then this one . . . and then this one . . . and then
the car . . . and then the house." Encourage the
person to set realistic, short-term goals within the
context of larger goals.

***"You can do* this!"**   You aim all of your optimis-
tic enthusiasm toward the accomplishment of one
goal. You may need to define that goal for the person
because a deeply troubled person may not be able to
put parameters around the task.

To the person just beginning a new business or
career, point out the specific tasks related to the first
day or first week on the job. Identify a goal that the

person can reach quickly. Help the person anticipate many small successes, all of which will lead toward a larger success.

"You can do this!" must, above all, reflect an attitude. It must be spoken with confidence and faith. "You can do this!" is the attitude that our parents had when they first encouraged us to rise up on our legs and walk. It's still a valid encouragement to give to those who need to develop their emotional legs and walk toward their full potential.

33 ♦ "One Thing I Really Admire About You Is . . ."

Many of us are taught from an early age not to think more highly of ourselves than we ought. Good advice. The key element, however, is "more highly" than we ought. It's quite acceptable to think of ourselves as we ought—to recognize our good points and value them. The opposite of self-pride is self-hate, which is just as destructive.

We need to learn to see our good qualities—not to get a big head but to see how to get ahead. We need to know what we have to work *with* before we tackle what we have to work *on*!

A discouraged individual most assuredly has lost sight of at least a portion of fine personal qualities. In most cases, discouragement goes hand in hand with a sense of inadequacy or failure. Encourage the person by pointing out strengths. What's good about the person? Conduct an inventory of assets—listing all of the positive strengths as a human being.

Natural talents What does the person seem to have a natural proclivity for? What comes easily? Which subjects in school were a snap? In what areas was success enjoyed in the past? Is he mechanically adept? Is she artistically inclined? Is he a wizard with words? Can she do long addition in her head?

Personal traits What about the person is attractive to others? Go beyond appearance. Does he have an ability to inspire confidence in others? Is she kind? Is he honest? Does she keep an open mind? Does he keep a secret? Does she think before she speaks? Is he easy to be around? Is she a giving, generous person?

Relational abilities What do you enjoy most about being with the person? Do you admire her thoughtful approach to solving problems? His big-with-gusto laugh? His enthusiasm? Her sensitivity to the needs of others? His willingness to be spontaneous? Her thoughtful appraisal of circumstances? The person's willingness to communicate?

General life skills Does the person handle problems well? Does he pay his bills on time? Does she follow through and do what she says she's going to do?

Each positive attribute is something to be noted and lauded. The more attributes on the list, the greater the encouragement!

34 ♦ "This Is My Special Friend"

Be sure to introduce your friends to one another.

Nothing is quite as immediately discouraging as having someone you're with engage in a conversation with someone you don't know and leave you standing alone in the conversational shadows.

This holds true for adults, teens, and children. For business relationships as well as friendships. In casual settings as well as those requiring formal protocol.

If you can't remember the person's name—which is sometimes the excuse given for not making an introduction—you can always point out something about the relationship you have with the person: "I see this face every Sunday at church. He is one of the most faithful parishioners in our congregation." Or "This is one of my fellow Scout parents. You should have seen us rolling bandages for an afternoon first-aid session!"

When introducing a person, tell about something uplifting.

Point to an Incident in Which the Person Helped You "This is my friend Grace. She is a graphic artist in our company, and I can't tell you how good she made our department look by the way she designed our latest product brochure." Or "This is Gary, my neighbor. He has a wonderful habit of mowing my front lawn each time he mows his. I now owe him 132 lawn mowings."

Point Out One or More Abilities or Skills

"This is my friend Kate—the finest copy editor I've ever met." Or "This is George from engineering. He's the one who solved the problem with the XK43 last year."

Point Out the Nature of Your Relationship

"This is Twila. We've been friends for more than two decades, and she still puts up with me. That tells you what patience and fortitude she has." Or "This is Tom. He's more than a second cousin. He's a real friend."

Point Out a Recent Accomplishment

"This is Ray. He's the only friend I have who has made a hole in one." Or "This is my friend Donald. He just recently issued his first solo recording of his original piano arrangements."

In introducing a person and finding something good to say about the person as a natural part of the process, you are saying, "This is a person of value to me and to the world. You're lucky to be meeting him or her." The person you are introducing can't help being encouraged!

35 ♦ "You Are One of a Kind"

In a society that creates more than 90 percent of all its products according to the principles of mass production and the desire for uniform components and interchangeable parts . . .

In a society where we feel intense pressure to look, dress, and talk for "success" within our peer groups . . .

In a society where "playing by the rules" tends to get us further than "coloring outside the lines" . . .

It's easy for us to lose sight of our originality. To feel like just another number. To get in a rut of self-identity. To get out of touch with our uniqueness. When that happens, our resulting malaise often has discouragement as a by-product.

Unique Advantages Encourage a person by pointing out that he or she is truly "one of a kind."

- No other set of fingerprints is just like his.
- No other voiceprint is just like hers.
- No other person has been born in precisely the same place or time, to the same set of parents, and in the same circumstances (not even a twin!).

And as a result . . .

- nobody has exactly the same opportunities in life.
- nobody will face an identical set of circumstances and problems.
- nobody will process information in exactly the same way.
- nobody will duplicate the person's work.
- nobody will have a body that processes nutrients and chemicals in precisely the same way.
- nobody will have the same impact on history at either the micro or the macro level.

Part of individuality lies in having a unique set of friends, a unique purpose in life, and a unique destiny. Part of our uniqueness is the never-before-trodden paths we choose to take around, through, and over our unique problems to get to our distinct achievements, accomplishments, and contributions.

Encourage a person by stating, "There has never been and there never will be another person just like you . . . and I'm glad for that. I count it a great privilege to know you in all your uniqueness!"

36 ◆ "You're Just Like a . . ."

Consider the names of professional sports teams. Many of them are rooted in the character trait of an animal or force of power, cunning, or skill—a trait we hope our team will display! Lions. Tigers. Angels. Bulls. Giants. Cardinals. Bullets. Sun. Sonics. Bears. Dolphins. Seahawks. Wonderful metaphors for the dreams and competition associated with winning!

Much of life is enhanced by metaphor. The discouraged person, however, tends not to see the world in vibrant color. The discouraged person tends to see the world—and herself—in a shade of murky gray. The encourager brings back the "color."

Vivid Portraits What is your discouraged friend like? How do you envision him? Be sure to picture him in his prime or ideal condition—not his present state of despair. Paint a word picture for him.

- Is his mind as sharp as a brand-new tack?
- Is she a rocket on the launchpad of her career, with the countdown just beginning?
- Are his values straight arrow, usually penetrating to the very center of an issue?
- Is she the tortoise who wins the race through

daily discipline and a constantly pressing desire to move forward?

• Is she a lioness protective of her pride of colleagues?
• Is she like a robin, quick to sing optimistically at the outset of a new season of growth?
• Is he like the sun streaming in a window after a long stormy night?
• Is she like the rapids of a mountain stream— bubbly, sparkling, finding joy even in life's rough moments?

Stop to think about your discouraged friend for a moment. Granted, he or she is wounded, temporarily down, momentarily bypassed or slowed. Refuse, however, to think of your friend as doomed, never to rise again. Choose to think of him as he once was and, even more important, how he can be—better than ever before.

Authentic Portraits Paint a word picture in your mind of your friend operating at peak performance, whole and full of energy in mind, spirit, body. Envision him relating to others in a way that promotes communication, progress, the creation of a better tomorrow. What metaphors come to mind? Write them down.

At a time when you can engage in quiet, thoughtful conversation with your friend, share your metaphors. You may need to explain them or elaborate upon them. Don't ask for a response. Simply paint your vision of the other person on the canvas of her mind: "To me, you are just like a . . ."

Mental Portraits   You might ask your friend to envision the picture you are about to describe. Ask him to see himself in the appropriate position or environment. Prompt her to put her face on the creature being described. Put the creatures in motion as you describe how the first robin arrives on the scene . . . the injured bird takes to flight again . . . the clouds roll away.

Each positive word picture you plant in the "mind's eye" of your discouraged friend will be like a tiny infusion of encouragement, with a time-release mechanism attached. Once planted, positive word pictures are difficult to erase completely.

37 ♦ "I Forgive You"

"The burden of them is intolerable." Such is the way the Book of Common Prayer describes our sins.

Guilt weighs heavy on the soul. It discourages and depresses us. We want to be what we aren't. We strive and fall short.

Three of the most encouraging words in the English language are these: "I forgive you."

Forgiveness frees.

Forgiveness restores.

Forgiveness heals.

Common Ground In regard to forgiveness, there are two points on which virtually all branches of Judaism and Christianity agree:

1. We do well when we forgive those who have wronged us. The person who willfully has injured another knows it (unless he is suffering from a memory defect). At some level he feels the burden of his deed. Our forgiving the person who has wronged us accomplishes two things simultaneously.

It removes us from standing in the way of the other person's confrontation of himself and his actions. We are no longer the "excuse" for the deed or the one against whom an act can be justified. In confronting himself and his evil acts, the person is in the right position for self-judgment and growth.

Forgiving others frees us from the negative impact of hatred on our souls, emotions, and bodies. All in all, forgiveness can prompt a genuine healing process at many levels!

2. We do well when we encourage others to face up to their errors, apologize for them, receive forgiveness of them—forgiving themselves in the process—and then move forward in their lives.

We can forgive others even if they don't ask us.

We can forgive others in a face-to-face meeting, by mail, or over the phone.

We can and should forgive simply, without elaboration:

- *"I accept your apology."*
- *"I forgive you."*
- *"I consider this forgiven and in the past."*

When a person bemoans his past failures, errors, mistakes, and sins against another person, you can say to him: "I don't hold this against you. Ask forgiveness of the one you have wronged and then forgive yourself. Move forward in your life and leave this behind you."

In forgiving others, you are saying, "I forgive you for not being perfect. I accept the fact that as a human being you will fail. Even so, I expect you to rise from your failures, dust yourself off, make amends as best as you can, and go on."

38 ♦ "You Are Not Alone"

The discouraged person often feels that nobody else has ever been where she's been, felt what she's felt, or thought what she's thought. Loneliness and discouragement often hang out together.

Encouragement is birthed when a person realizes that she is not the only one on the planet to have encountered a specific circumstance or problem . . . and lived to tell about it.

Support Groups If a person you know is discouraged about a habit that he has failed thus far to break—but would like to break—encourage him to find a support group of people engaged in a similar struggle. It might be a stop-smoking group, a dieting group, an Alcoholics Anonymous group, or any other of a large number of stop-it-anonymously associations. In virtually all cases, these groups are for those who recognize they have a problem, desire to solve the problem, and have faced the fact that they are having difficulty solving the problem on their own. The "collective will" of the group helps to bolster flagging willpower, and medical support systems frequently are available to help with the physical and psychological aspects of addiction.

Support groups generally have one thing in common: the opportunity to share personal stories. As these stories are shared, the discouraged person may come to feel as if he's hearing "same song, multiple verse" recitations of his problem. As that awareness emerges, feelings of isolation and loneliness tend to dissipate. As individuals share what has and hasn't worked for them in solving a problem, your friend will gain constructive information.

In addition to support groups, the "stories of others" are also available in testimonial books or via movies, videotapes, or guest speakers.

Workshops are another good place in which to find clusters of people with similar problems. Workshops are generally aimed at problem solving or information sharing.

In many ways, a church is an enlarged support group. Its pervasive theme is "You are not alone." In your struggles with doubt and sin, in your attempts to communicate with God, in your frustrations with life and your concerns for the hereafter . . . "you are not alone."

You can always say to your discouraged friend, "I know you are not alone. How do I know? Because I can find at least ten people who have been through what you've been through. Will you join me in seeking them out?"

The Buddy System   Let's assume for a moment that a person does have a unique problem. To be certain, each problem has unique aspects and angles to it since each person and each relationship is unique. Even so, you can encourage the person that she is not alone. You are choosing to be there in the midst of the problem with her!

Furthermore, even though you may not have experienced the precise problem that your friend is facing, you have undoubtedly felt the same emotions he is feeling! The "fear" of an impending divorce is not unlike the "fear" of an impending job layoff or the "fear" of the impending death of a grandparent. Fear of loss, change in relationship, or isolation is still FEAR.

We've all been angry. We've all been frustrated with our inabilities. We've all lost something dear to us. We've all failed at something we considered important. We've all struggled against odds we don't like. We are human beings—creatures of the same species!

You may not be able to advise a person from your experience or training about how to avoid a problem or live through it, but you can always assure the person that you are present to "walk through the emotions" with him.

Robert Fulghum, in his famous essay entitled "All I Really Need to Know I Learned in Kindergarten," cites as one basic principle for life, "When you go out into the world, it is best to hold hands and stick together." That's good advice for all of life and encouraging news to a friend walking a path of discouragement.

39 ◆ "I Believe God Loves You, and I Do, Too"

We all long to be loved with a love that is unconditional, pure, and generously applied.

The ancient Greeks had a name for such love—*agape*. *Agape* is the love attributed to God. It is divine love that flows without restraint and without the lusts of *eros* (sexual love) or the human conditions and limitations of *phileo* (brotherly love). It goes beyond the love of one's family. It is pervasive, pumping from the very heartbeat of the divine.

Within each of us is a seed of *agape* waiting to be kindled for the benefit of another. With that flame lighted we can say genuinely, "I love you, even as I believe God loves you."

Your Love For many people, the idea that you might love them is far more readily accepted than the idea that God might love them. The notion of a harsh, judgmental, ready-to-zap-you God is pervasive. The discouraged person often feels condemned in some cosmic way—as if it's his "fate" to be doomed by circumstances or strangled by life's woes. It can be of great encouragement to hear from another, "I believe God is merciful. He loves. He created you in order to love you." One of the most encouraging things you can ever do for another person is to open her up to the idea that divine mercy and love are extended to her.

God's Love For others, the notion that God loves them is more acceptable than the idea that any human being could or does. For these individuals, God is often perceived as having the "job" of loving. His love is often viewed as a universal entity poured out in a generalized manner, as syrup over a hefty stack of unidentifiable human pancakes. What an encouragement for such a person to hear, "I love you because God sent me to love you. Here are my arms around you. Think of them as God's arms. Here is my shoulder to cry on. Think of it as His. I am saying, 'I love you.' Think of the words as coming from His mouth."

To the person who has never heard the words . . .

To the person who hasn't heard them in a long time . . .

To the person who is wounded, hurting, and in deep emotional pain . . .

No words are more soothing than these: "God has put a piece of His infinite love for you in my heart, and so I say to you today, 'I love you. I believe God loves you, too.' "

Love is at the root of all encouragement. It helps at times to identify it as such and bring it out in the open.

40 ♦ "You ARE Growing"

The discouraged individual rarely has a sense of her progress—in personal growth, in relationships, in career, finances, or abilities. The "encourager" sees growth and calls attention to it!

Specific Changes In citing positive changes, be specific. For example, say, "You know, a few months ago, an encounter like that would have had you in tears. Today, you faced that with an entirely different attitude."

Say, "Six weeks ago you couldn't walk more than ten minutes without being exhausted. Today, you walked twenty-three minutes. That's more than 100 percent improvement in just six weeks!"

Deal with long enough time periods so that significant progress can be noted. Many people who are recovering from an injury—physical or emotional—have ups and downs, often two steps forward and one step back. Point out trends over weeks and months rather than give daily progress reports. Very few of us can note a 10 percent change in anything, much less a 1 or 2 percent change, and yet, that is how most change occurs—one percentile at a time.

Cite specific examples of . . .

• interpersonal behavior.

"This time last year, you would have blown up in anger at hearing a statement like that. Now you're finding a constructive way of making a response!"

• physical attributes.

"This time three months ago, you weighed twenty-four pounds more than you do today. At this rate, you'll arrive at your goal by summer!"

• emotions that have lessened in intensity.

"You haven't cried for four days? Why, this time ninety days ago, you were in tears at least twenty times a day."

• insights.

"A year ago you would have just swept that information under the rug. Now you are facing facts squarely rather than suppressing evidence."

• new habits.

"Six months ago you were drinking five or six cocktails after work to unwind. Today you're drinking a soda."

• new skills.

"You didn't even know how to turn on a computer two months ago and look at all you can do today."

Once a person has developed a mind-set of "I'm sick" (or "I'm depressed" or "I'm anything . . ." except whole or getting better), it's very difficult for that person to see growth toward a better future. You may find it helpful to discuss with the discouraged person his definition of health or wholeness. Ask . . .

• *"What are you looking for as a sign of health?"*
• *"To what level of health are you anticipating you will recover?"*
• *"What do you think 'wholeness' will entail for you?"*

Goals   Help the person set specific goals for reaching better health and wholeness. Set goals with different time frames—for example, thirty-day goals, ninety-day goals, this-time-next-year goals. Ask . . .

• *"What do you hope you will be able to do next month that you can't do now?"*
• *"What would you like to be able to do within three months?"*
• *"What would you like to be happening in your life this time next year?"*

Write down these goals for future reference and discussion. Even if the person hasn't fully obtained a goal, point out the level to which success has been reached.

At times, the discouraged person is so depressed that she can't envision "how" goals can be reached. She simply cannot see what she must do to get from A to B. In these cases, help the person break down goals into detailed lists of things to do. Help the person plan regimens, menus, timetables, payment plans, schedules, and so forth—or recommend experts who can help with short- and long-term goal setting and strategic personal planning.

41 ◆ "I Like You"

Your friend is deeply discouraged after losing his job, his wife in a bitter divorce, and his father in a six-month period. You can't seem to cheer him up. He has a counterargument or negative reaction to every positive or uplifting thing you say. What can you do?

100 Reasons Purchase a cloth-bound blank book that has about a hundred pages and title the volume *100 Reasons Why I Like You*. Here are some examples of reasons to include:

- I like your crooked-mouth grin.
- I like your green plaid shirt.
- I like the fact that you never get tired of going out for enchiladas.
- I like the way you always keep your car clean.
- I like the fact that you would find a joke like this funny (and clip out a joke and paste it on the page).

Conclude with, "I like the fact that we're good enough friends that you won't feel you have to respond with one hundred reasons why you like me!"

(That will get him off the hook in case he thinks you expect a reply in kind.)

The discouraged person frequently sees himself as unlikable, untouchable, unlovable, and worth very little. Point out to him that it just ain't so!

42 ♦ "You May Be Down, But You're Not Out"

A discouraged person tends to foresee a future exactly like the terrible today. She can't see how she will ever feel better than she feels right now. She can't envision how she will ever be able to function better than she can this day.

Terrific Tomorrows At that point the encourager needs to say, "Listen. I agree with you that now is not nice. I fully expect, however, that a tomorrow in the not-too-distant future is going to be terrific."

Don't let a person say, "Well, I guess I'll always be an invalid." Respond, "Hmmm. I don't agree. I think you'll be valid. Not _in_valid. You still have a great contribution to make to this world, and here's how I see it" (and proceed to cite specific things you feel certain the person can and will contribute to the family, church, social group, or community or to you as a friend).

Don't let a person say, "I'll probably never find somebody to love me." Respond, "I beg your pardon. Since when am I nobody?" Talk about all of the good traits of the person that make her attractive to a future mate.

Redefinition Even though you may be responding with a lighthearted answer, you aren't really making light of the situation. You are causing interference in the way the person regards himself. You're forcing the person to take a second look at what he is saying about his life and to redefine his outlook.

Always point out specific ways in which you see the person acting and speaking as someone who is whole and healthy, lovable and vibrant; someone who can make a contribution.

The discouraged person is very often depleted of energy, emotional reserves, ideas, or creativity. The concept of "depleted," however, is a much more positive one than that of "depressed" or "despondent." Depletion carries with it the notion that the container can be filled again. Energy can return. Creativity can resurface. Emotions can well up again to full strength.

If a person says to you, "I'm depressed," encourage her to say instead, "I'm depleted." Focus on ways in which the person can be *re*pleted—filled up again with the good inner stuff that makes for strength and verve. What's missing? What needs to be added? Where can you go and what can you do to regain what has been lost?

As an encourager, you must help your discouraged friend redefine himself.

43 ♦ "Something Good Is About to Happen"

Sometimes a person gets so accustomed to hearing bad news that he can't hear good news when it comes. He seems permanently braced for the worst . . . and in that state, he usually misses out on many of life's small, sterling moments.

Seek the Good   The truth is, something good is always just about to happen. It all depends on how you define *good*.

- The morning sunrise
- Crisp cereal with ice-cold milk and a mug of steaming coffee
- Warm gloves on a cold morning
- The on-time bus
- The bright colors of the flowers at the corner flowerstand
- The chimes of the neighborhood church
- The lack of bills in the mailbox
- The reflection of blue sky and white clouds in the puddle left after the thunderstorm
- The wagging tail of a puppy

- Late-afternoon sun streaming through the window
- The new contact you made . . . the new client who phones . . . the new person you met at lunch
- The hug of a small child
- A hot bubble bath

All are a delight if you choose to see them as such.

Magnify the Good Good things happen to us all. It's up to us to magnify those moments, be enthusiastically thankful for them, savor them, and hold them gently in memory.

If we discount them, we lose a sense of life's balance when bad events come our way, which they most assuredly will.

The discouraged person frequently loses sight of the fact that life is a mix of good and bad, in varying proportions. It's never entirely one way or the other. And much of what we experience is actually neutral. Most events are "good" or "bad" only if we so label them.

Life's events are life's events. In nearly all cases, they have only the value we give them.

The encourager helps the discouraged person to discover the good moments, good things, and good encounters in each day.

44 ◆ "Don't Miss Your Exit Sign"

Today most people complain about the stress of being stuck in life's fast lane. They tend to feel they are whizzing by moments that they suspect might be worth a second look, accelerator floorboarded as they attempt to get to some destination.

The fast-forward person can have a sense of loss, discouraged about what she might be missing. Many top executives voice a wistful longing for a simpler place and time, and at the same time, they admit frustration at their inability to envision how to pay for life's necessities with less effort or a less hurried pace.

Many people feel they have no control over their daily regimen, much less their futures. They have a feeling that life is happening to them and that they have no power to change their pace, their track, their relationships.

To those discouraged persons in danger of becoming stressed out or burned out by the fast pace they are moving on life's interstate highway, the encouraging word may well be, "Don't miss your turn-off."

The encourager points out . . .

- *"It's never too late to change things."*
- *"No one way of life is better than any other, except as you define it to be so."*
- *"You have the ability to change."*
- *"You have the inner fortitude to make a change."*

New Roads An exit is never to be regarded, in this analogy, as death, divorce, or any negative path —no, not even a detour! The exit should always be viewed as the passage to a different road—one with new scenery, a new pace, new opportunities, new secrets worth exploring, new way stations.

In very practical terms, the new road might be

- a new place of service.
- a new job or career.
- a new city.
- a new friend, mentor, student, or associate.
- a new habit or set of habits.
- a new set of priorities.
- a new commitment.
- a new level of involvement at your church.

Sometimes just recognizing that exits are there— on freeways as well as on backroads—is sufficient to help a person feel encouraged that he isn't locked into a future that's the same as today.

45 ♦ "I Don't Believe You Need That Crutch"

The discouraged person often surrounds himself with props, feeling unable to succeed without them. Sometimes those props become the cause of further discouragement. When that happens, a vicious addictive cycle is established. This is especially true when the addiction includes a dependency on mood-altering chemicals.

People may start out using drugs, but in the long run, the drugs use up people—using up their energy and ability, using up their money and time, using up their potential and, eventually, using up their lives!

Break the Cycle The encourager says, "I believe you can make it without an artificial support system."

- *"I believe you can sleep through the night without the aid of a pill."*
- *"I believe you can succeed without getting high."*
- *"I believe you can relax without a drink."*
- *"I believe you can make it through the day without nicotine."*
- *"I believe you can learn to handle life without a tranquilizer."*

This is not to deny the value of medications when they are necessary to restore normal bodily function and when they are taken as prescribed. It is to say that no person should ever be made to feel—or come to feel—the need to rely permanently on mood-altering chemicals for emotional well-being. It is to say that no person should be allowed to become addicted to chemicals out of a desire to create a perception of reality that is forever comfortable. The reality created by drugs is nearly always a distorted one. True reality requires an ability to deal with tragedies —accommodating the unchangeable and changing what can be changed and, above all, recognizing the difference.

Retrain In many cases, achieving a life without chemical crutches requires more than courage and a willingness to try—it takes intensive retraining. Learning to reface a reality once escaped requires "rethinking" life and altering one's perceptions, resetting one's goals, reevaluating one's values and priorities, and replacing unhealthy habits.

The encouraging friend says, "I believe you can experience a new, more healthy, more fulfilling reality without chemical props . . . if you'll try."

46 ◆ "Things Don't Need to Stay This Way"

Most of us would like to change something about our lives. New Year's resolutions are evidence of that. Nearly everybody makes at least one.

The discouraged person often feels, however, that he cannot change—that it is beyond his willpower to effect change or to do anything about the circumstances. The discouraged person frequently feels trapped by a lack of resolve and an inability to move.

The encourager declares, "You have the power, authority, and responsibility to change what you don't like in your life."

Things Can Change It is true that the person may not be able to make the change on her own. In 99 percent of all cases, that is likely to be so! None of us can live successfully as an island, self-sufficient unto ourselves.

Our power to change our lives is nearly always manifest in our power to ask for, seek out, and avail ourselves of the help offered by others. We are rarely in a position where we cannot say, *"I want to see things changed. I feel helpless to bring about this change by myself. Please help me!"*

The encourager proclaims to the despondent person:

- *"Believe things can change."*
- *"Admit you can't bring about the change on your own."*
- *"Put yourself into a position of getting help."*
- *"Call out for assistance."*
- *"Surround yourself with people who are willing and able to help you and to give you reliable, valid advice."*

Sometimes discouraged people feel so trapped that they can't even identify or define the change they would like to occur. They know only that they are miserable. In those cases, you might encourage the person by saying,

- *"Admit you're miserable."*
- *"Get help from someone who can help you isolate exactly what is causing you to feel so bad."*
- *"Don't run until you know where you're running."*

Growth Through Change "Running away" won't solve the problem; the better choice is to run toward a solution or toward a new set of better circumstances.

The encourager believes that change is possible and that for every person, periodic change can be an opportunity for growth. We shouldn't change just for the sake of change, but we should expect change as a natural part of growth. Change is desirable for us all

—assuming that change leads us toward a better goal and a better reality.

The real bottom line, then, is to say to the discouraged person,

> *"You can grow out of this into something better. It is your God-given nature as a human being to grow. It is part of the potential built into your human spirit. Seek the highest and best of life and eternity and grow toward it. Change will happen as you grow. Embrace those changes that come with growth, and allow for transformation in your life."*

47 ◆ "Isn't This Good?"

Fleeting are the moments of bliss in life. How encouraging to have someone point them out to us and to share them with us in a spirit of abandon!

A dear friend who faces life with that type of enthusiasm frequently asserts, "Oh, isn't this *g-o-o-d!*" The only possible answer is a hearty "yes and forever amen!"

Enthusiasm The encourager enthusiastically proclaims what pleases him or her, regardless of time, place, or audience. The encourager underscores dozens of daily moments and marks them with a positive exclamation point!

- *"What delicious soup!"* Oh, so g-o-o-d.
- *"Have you ever seen such a beautiful bouquet?!"* Oh, isn't it g-o-o-d.
- *"Aren't you glad you live in a country where freedom reigns!"* Oh, yes, it's g-o-o-d.
- *"Doesn't it make your heart glad when you see parents love their children like that?"* Yes, it makes my heart feel g-o-o-d.
- *"Aren't you excited about the new plans!"* Yes, there's great g-o-o-d ahead.

- *"Isn't he a great guy!"* Yes, he's a g-o-o-d guy with which to share life.
- *"Aren't you glad you know her?"* Yes, a thousand g-o-o-d yeses.
- *"Isn't it a great day to be alive!"* Yes, its very, very, very g-o-o-d.

Praise   By embracing all of life's very best, the encourager sings a silent but glorious doxology:

> *Praise God, from whom all blessings flow.*
> *Praise Him, all creatures here below.*
> *Praise Him above, you heavenly host.*
> *Praise Father, Son, and Holy Ghost.*

The encourager chooses to believe that the world really is a great big wonderful place and that each life can be wonderful.

48 ♦ "You Have Options"

Discouraged people often feel they've reached the end of the road rather than see a situation as a Y in the path of life.

You can encourage a person who feels that she has run into a brick wall or careened into a dead-end alley by engaging in a straightforward business-style planning session to explore options.

1. Declare Your Belief that the Person Has Options Everybody does at every juncture of life. There's never just one way to do things. In fact, there's rarely a "best way" that is obviously superior to all other "good ways." The "ideal world" is rarely available for occupancy.

Has your friend received a pink slip at work?
This is the time to explore options!

2. Identify as Many Options as Possible Employ brainstorming techniques. Freewheel your ideas. Let nothing be dismissed as too absurd or too farfetched.

Your friend might get another job . . . move to a city where there are more jobs . . . start a business or consulting firm . . . run away to Hawaii . . . sit down and cry . . . contact an employment agency . . . call every friend and ask for help . . . prepare a resume and send it to fifty firms . . . and the list goes on!

3. Explore the Various Options and Evaluate Each One

What are its desirable outcomes, its feasibility, and its cost in terms of personal and material resources? Identify what appears to be the weakness of each option and any constraints, qualifiers, or risks associated with it.

Let's assume your friend chooses the option of getting another job as the best way to stay alive, support her family, and feel fulfilled in life.

4. Rank the Options

Choose Plan A, Plan B, and so forth. You may be able to cluster several options under one plan.

Preparing a resume, networking friends, and contacting an employment agency are all ways of pursuing the larger goal of getting another job.

5. Define the Way to Implement the Best Option

Again, there's always more than one way to turn an option into a reality. Consider timing, methods, and all of the prerequisites that may need

to be in place for success (including people, resources, information, advance publicity, location).

*Your friend decides to call five friends a day for the
first week and follow up with notes of appreciation to
them the next week . . . to have a resume ready by
Wednesday . . . and to make an appointment with
an employment agency before 10:00 A.M. on Monday.*

What happens if the option chosen doesn't take
you where you thought it would? What happens if
Plan A doesn't succeed?
There are always more options to consider!

49 ◆ "This Won't Last Forever"

Nothing stays the same forever—no matter how bad it is.

That's encouraging news to the person who feels as if no progress is being made, no matter how hard he is working or how much he is trying.

- Recessions are turned around.
- Decisions are reached.
- Breakthroughs happen.
- New ideas spring forth.
- Circumstances alter.
- New discoveries are made.

No Condition Is Permanent As an encourager, you can help a discouraged person rephrase what she perceives to be a permanent condition into a transitional or temporary one:

- *"You're not divorced or widowed. You're presently single."*
- *"You're not bankrupt. You're starting out on a new business path."*
- *"You're not unemployed. You're in career transition."*

- *"You're not homeless. You're in the process of moving into a new home."*

Facing Eternity The biggest change of all, of course, will come to each of us in the form of death. For the person diagnosed with a terminal illness . . . for the elderly person who feels weaker with each passing month . . . for the person struggling with intense pain that grows worse . . . there's great encouragement in believing, "This won't last forever. There's a better future awaiting."

On days when a person is weary of work, tired of trying, and fed up with frustrations, she can take delight in thinking about an everlasting future in which all work counts, all friendships are rich, all goals are reached, and all decisions are correct. The hope of heaven encourages.

50 ♦ "You Are Precious Beyond Price"

Value means having purpose, a reason for being, a contribution to make, a marker to place in time and space.

The encourager says to another, "You are precious beyond price. You have value!"

"You're Irreplaceable" Nobody can ever take your place—on this earth and, more specifically, in my life. Nobody else can be what you are, do what you do. Nobody else will ever say precisely what you say, give what you give, create what you create, or leave behind what you leave behind. Nobody else can fill your niche.

"You're Incredible" You are fearfully and wonderfully made. You know just what to say and do to meet the need. You have abilities and potential that are so fantastic they can't be measured.

"You're on Your Way" You have a bright future ahead. You have blessings yet to be experienced and wonderful experiences yet to live. You're headed in the right direction. Your values are intact, your courage is inspiring, and your enthusiasm is contagious.

"And I Count It a Privilege to Call You My Friend" I feel blessed that our paths have crossed. I feel awed that we have the joy of knowing each other. I feel comforted in knowing that you are in the universe. I cherish your friendship and pledge you mine in return. And I anticipate with joy the possibility that we will know each other forever.

What wonderful words of encouragement!

To be an encourager is to know you have value and to be unabashedly bold in declaring the value of another—whether that other person is a family member, friend, coworker, fellow worshiper, team member, club associate, casual acquaintance, or passing stranger.

Parting Principles

51 ◆ Some People Won't Receive Your Encouragement

No matter what you say or do . . .
   No matter how often you try . . .
   No matter what methods you use . . .
   No matter how sincere you are . . .
   Some people will *not* receive the encouragement you attempt to give them.

It Takes Two Encouragement has a lot in common with the tango, the teeter-totter, and the perpetuation of the species . . . it takes two for success.

To receive your words and deeds of encouragement, a person must be at least partially willing to be encouraged by you. He must be at least open to the idea of encouragement. She must crack open the door of her heart, mind, and will and let you in. He must be at least 1 percent willing to try.

If she isn't, you can't.

Don't Yield to Discouragement Don't let your failure to encourage another person result in your own discouragement! Don't let the pervasive discouragement of one who refuses to be encouraged contaminate your hope and joy or infect your enthusiasm for life.

Sometimes you won't be able to reach the de-pressed, despondent, or discouraged friend in need. Someone with a different personality or way of com-municating may be more effective. Sometimes you won't have the information, skills, or experience re-quired. Sometimes the timing won't be right.

- Do what you can do.
- Help in all the ways you know to help.
- Say what you know to say.
- And if you receive no response, move on . . . because a second principle is equally true. Read about it on the next page.

52 ◆ Everybody Needs Encouragement

You may not be able to see the person's problem.

He may seem to be on top of the world.

She may appear to have it all or at least have all it takes.

He may look in perfect health.

She may exhibit great faith, great emotional strength, and great enthusiasm for life.

He may exude optimism and joy, faith and hope.

But, the truth is, everybody needs encouragement. And not just some of the time. All of the time!

Instill Hope Nobody has all of the confidence needed to grow to full potential . . . all the hope stimulated to face tomorrow . . . or all the resources required to further personal growth. No matter who you encounter, the person needs to hear the encouraging words that only you can say.

Don't limit your words of encouragement to persons you feel are down and out or at least lower on the emotional health totem pole than you are. Don't withhold your words and deeds of encouragement from someone because you feel he doesn't "need" it. He does.

Adopt the perspective that you are going to look

for ways in which to encourage every person who crosses your path—in some way, with some word or deed, anticipating some positive result in that person's life and in your own.

Receive Hope   At the same time, be open to being encouraged. Let the words of encouragement you speak be heard by your own two ears. Be receptive to the words of encouragement you hear coming your way. Take them into your being and let them take root.

The encouragement you mete out tends to come back to you in like measure. The more you receive encouragement, seek all the more to give it. Give great encouragement, and be greatly encouraged. Encouragement can become a cycle in your life that generates joy, promotes wholeness, and gives strength—to others as well as to yourself.

Encourage someone today! You'll both be glad you did!